Wal

WONDERFUL WIGAN

By

Cliff Peters

© Copyright 2021 Cliff Peters

All rights reserved

This book shall not, by way of trade or otherwise, be lent, re-sold, hired out, or otherwise circulated without the prior consent of the copyright holder or the publisher in any form of binding or cover other than that in which it is published and without a similar condition including this condition being imposed on the subsequent purchaser. The use of its contents in any other media is also subject to the same conditions.

ISBN: 978-1-913839-08-6

MMXXI

A CIP catalogue record for this book
is available from the British Library

Published by
ShieldCrest Publishing Ltd.,
Aylesbury, Buckinghamshire,
HP18 0TF England
Tel: +44 (0) 333 8000 890
www.shieldcrest.co.uk

Acknowledgements:

My constant companion throughout the compilation of the book has been my wife, Lynn. We took many wrong turns and climbed quite a few fences in our quest to find new walks, but thoroughly enjoyed it all. Thank you.

Though we could not meet for our walks during lockdown, the 'Walking Chums' (our WhatsApp group title), were instrumental in formulating many of the walks. Alan, Dave, Ian, John (the book's resident historian) and I have revelled in discovering hidden parts of Wigan, whilst at the same time putting the world to rights every Tuesday. Our discussions ranged from politics to news, religion and every conceivable sport to absolute rubbish (mostly rubbish)! We also somehow contrived to consume more calories on each walk than we expended, which was baffling.

Introduction

Probably the first thought that might occur to a reader from outside Wigan, is: 'Why would anyone actually *want* to go walking in Wigan?'. Perhaps the general perception being that the town consists of countless rows of terraced houses set amongst numerous factories and the unsightly remains of the once-prolific mining and textile industries. This might once have been true!

Modern Wigan and its surroundings are miles away from this perception, and I'm confident that this little book will go a long way to proving this. The walks outlined here include many of the popular beauty spots in the town, which I think are as picturesque and inspiring as anywhere in the country.

We Wiganers have long appreciated our well-known beauty spots, such as 'Fairy Glen', Borsdane Wood, Pennington Flash, Worthington Lakes, and of course Haigh Hall and the Plantations. These have provided tastes of the rural countryside surrounding Wigan for countless years, mixing history with nature.

Our area has a superb canal network criss-crossing the town. This has been very well maintained, providing access to both the sailing and the walking fraternity. The town's mining legacy has seen the creation of several nature reserves spread throughout the area, which provide a multitude of pathways through beautifully forested areas, with an abundance of waterways and the accompanying wildlife. These vast areas cover huge expanses of Bickershaw, Ashton, Hindley, Standish, Aspull and Leigh, all once thriving mining areas. I'm sure you will come to agree that the Wigan area certainly has a lot to offer.

From a personal point of view, my love of walking began with trips to the Yorkshire Dales, and the Lake District (as I'm sure was the case with many people). When my wife and I bought a caravan on the edges of Settle, our long weekends always included a couple of walks in the 'Dales' or Trough of Bowland. Then, as retirement approached, and we sold the caravan, mid-week walks with some old rugby mates began to bring about a realisation of what I'd been missing. Our walks were basically confined to the environs of Wigan, and we all became increasingly amazed at the fantastic walks we were discovering.

Then the Covid-19 epidemic arrived. That led to a nationwide lockdown in March 2020; although it was a tragic period for many people, in me, it began to cement the idea for this book. I was determined to use the daily allotted exercise quota to the full, and proceeded to walk every day (very often with Lynn, my wife). I also set myself a remit to fully discover our lovely town, and its surrounding areas. I covered over 600 extremely enjoyable miles during this three-month period, discovering new pathways and experiences every day.

During these exploratory walks, I became enthralled at the abundance of nature that thrives in the town. I came across roe and fallow deer; weasel; hare and rabbit; and squirrel by the hundred. I saw and heard countless songbirds (including the elusive kingfisher), several varieties of waterfowl, and birds of prey (great crested grebe and marsh harriers among them). I was also really surprised by the number of thriving and well-stocked stables in the borough (maybe Wigan should be twinned with Goodwood?). Wigan has proved to be a great surprise and source of pleasure even to a resident of 65 years, and it still continues to be so. I hope you will eventually be of the same opinion.

Whilst none of the walks illustrated in this book are particularly demanding, it is advisable to wear appropriate clothing and boots when you undertake them. A flask and a light snack might also come in useful. You should also allow ample time to complete the walks in daylight. I have attempted, where possible, to avoid walking on major roads, but it is often necessary to spend short lengths of time on them, to link up tracks. I've also, you will notice, attempted to include a local 'watering hole' near to the start/end of the walk. Nothing like a well-earned pint after a satisfying and tiring walk!

CONTENTS

Introduction

Walks

1	Borsdane and Kirkless Woods	1
2	Hindley Green, Daisy Hill and Westleigh	5
3	Abram, Bickershaw and Hindley Green	9
4	Flashes, Locks and Rugby Clubs	12
5	Adlington and Worthington Lakes	15
6	Fairies, Pheasants and Football	19
7	Bridgewater Canal and Pennington Flash	23
8	Water, water everywhere (Viridor Woods and the Canal)	27
9	Wigan's Royalty Walk	30
10	Standish Circular	34
	The author	37

Key

Walk route

Major road

Track

Railway line

Canal or river

Other water

Pub

Woodland

Building

Walk Locations

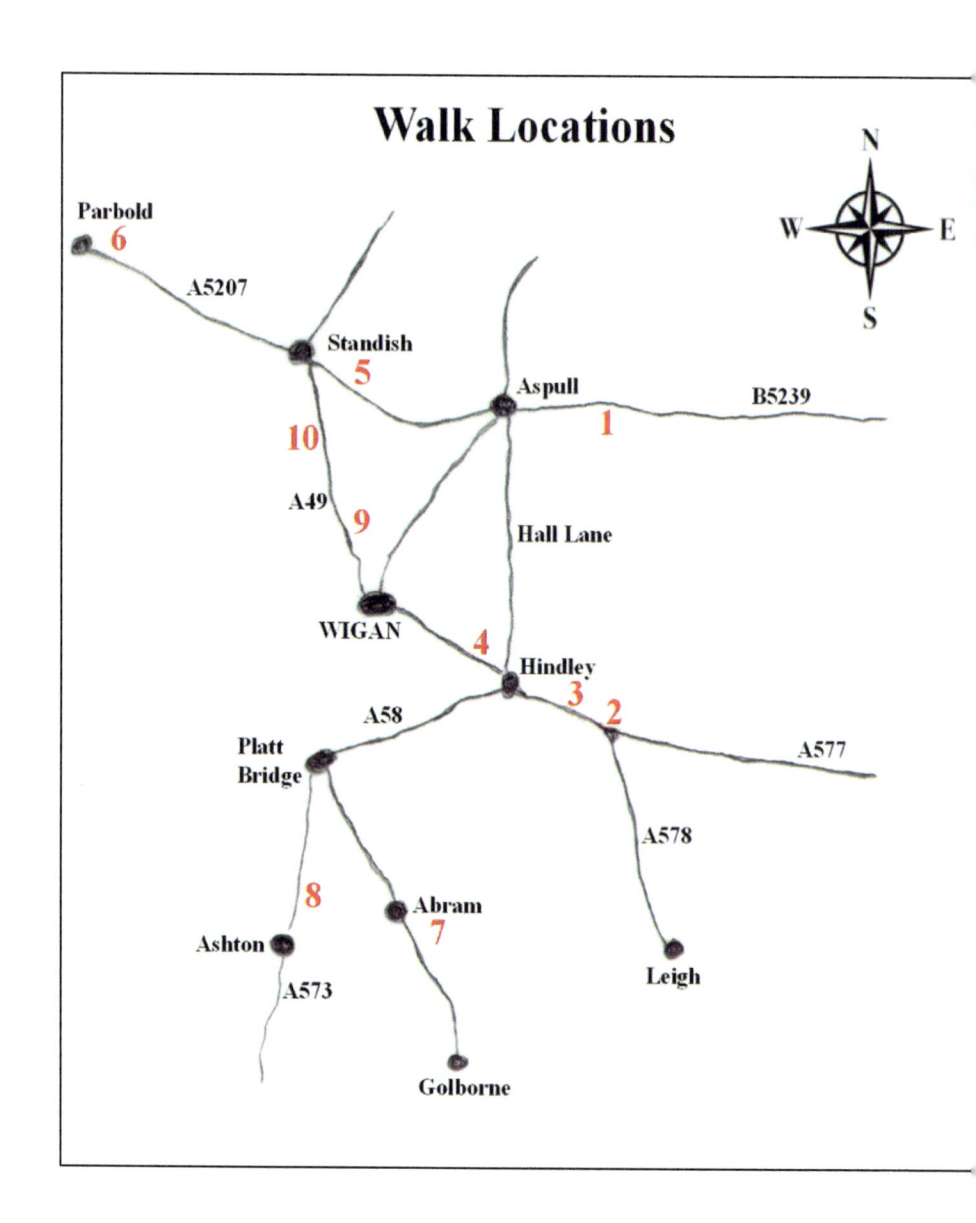

Walk 1

Borsdane and Kirkless Woods

Distance: 6 miles
Time: 2.5 hours

Terrain: Very good tracks and footpaths throughout, and pretty flat as well.

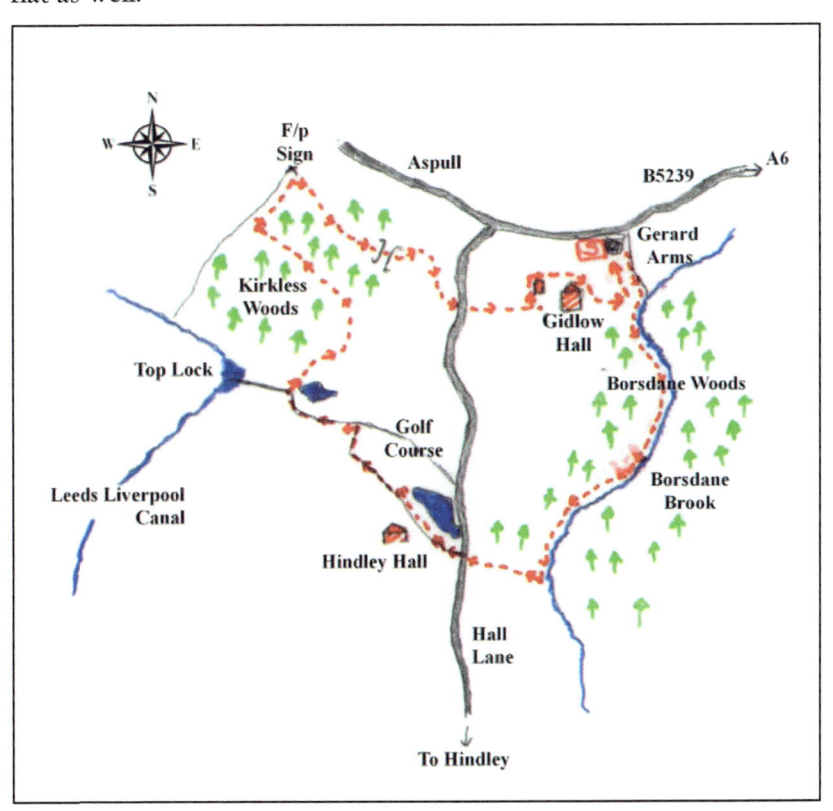

This wonderful walk not only passes through two delightful woodland areas, but also crosses one of the town's oldest and most scenic golf courses.

We begin on the car park of the Gerard Arms on Bolton Road, heading from Aspull towards the A6. Turn right out of the car park, and follow the street down to the bottom, where you will arrive at the entrance of Borsdane Wood (the new housing you pass on your left is built on the old site of Dicconson Mill, which burnt down in 1990). Go down the track and cross a metal bridge to enter the woods (note the little 'fairy' door carved into the oak tree as you cross). You now have a two-mile stroll through this beautiful, ancient woodland. Take your time; take in the smell of wild garlic. Make sure to keep your eyes open along the left-hand edges for the often-seen deer near the water's edge and observe the abundance of birdlife (nuthatch, great spotted woodpeckers, chaffinch, robin and blue tits abound).

Before you know it, you will begin to approach the Hindley end of the wood, and as you spot a large picnic bench in a clearing, there is a footpath sign in a fence on the right. Pass through the stile, climbing a rough track overlooking a glorious glen on its right, which was covered in bluebells in the spring. Keep to this path, and eventually emerge onto Hall Lane in Hindley. Cross immediately, and follow the footpath sign on the opposite side, which passes through the Hindley Hall Golf Club (Be aware of the first tee on your left, as the golfers drive across the path... well, some do!).

You will pass the ancient Hindley Hall (built in 1811 by Alexander Leigh), now the clubhouse, on your left. Continue, and a few hundred yards further, the path swings to the right, and ends at a metal gate. Go through, and turn left up the wide track, past a row of terraced houses. Upon reaching some more substantial properties, bear right, and look for a private fishing lodge on your right, and a footpath sign pointing right (you are only a few hundred yards from 'Top Lock' at this point, but if you reach it you have missed the sign… go back). You soon see another waymarker sign on your right. Take this and follow the grassy path, as it swings left then right around a wooded hill; you are now in Kirkless Wood.

Carry on around the wooded hill. You will reach a fence, and soon come across another footpath sign at a gate. Take the level path on your right (the steps on the other path are manageable, but the undulations along the top of the hill are rather dangerous). Follow the narrow track through the light woodland, until you come to a wooden bridge crossing a stream. Cross the bridge and continue in the same direction on a path that follows alongside open pastures that usually contain several horses. At the top of this path, another path crosses it, and you are turning right (Aspull R.U. Club, is to the left). This track continues past the farm, and again reaches Hall Lane.

A hundred yards to your right there is a signpost on the opposite side of the road. Cross to this and go over the unusual stile in the fence to progress up the field. At the top of the field, there is another stile at the side of the N.W.W.A Treatment Works. Pass round the edge of these works, heading right upon reaching a path. If you look to your right as you pass the other end of the waterworks, you will see the impressive Gidlow Hall, behind some massive iron gates, and a conifer hedge (this Hall dates back to 1574, and was originally built for Robert de Gidlow, a local aristocrat). Proceed past some bungalows, and some very new housing, then follow a narrow entry and a stile onto a narrow track that winds through a small, wooded area, and out onto a car park. Turn left and follow the street back up to the Gerard Arms.

Gidlow Hall

Walk 2

Hindley Green, Daisy Hill and Westleigh

Distance: 5 miles
Time: 2 hours

Terrain: Decent paths and dirt tracks. A few places can get muddy after heavy rain.

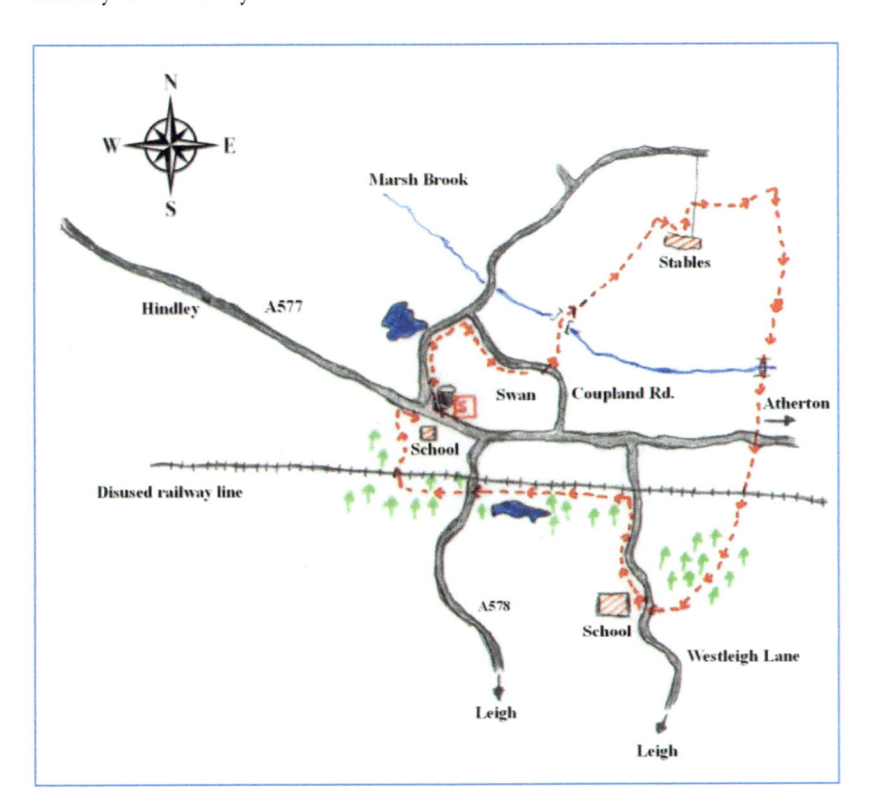

A very comfortable and pretty walk along some lovely country lanes, and the remains of the old Wigan/Leigh railway line. You depart from the Swan Hotel on Atherton Road in Hindley Green. Leave the car park at the rear of the pub, and progress up Swan Lane. Where the road bends to the right you pass a gym (formerly the government skills centre), and then shortly after, turn right along Coupland Road, through an industrial estate (apologies for the half mile or so of not very attractive road walking, but it will soon prove to be worthwhile). After about five hundred yards look for a wooden gate on the left-hand side and go through to enter grassland.

Continue past a large, fenced house, cross a bridge over a stream, and carry on along the left of the hedge up the next two fields. These were both planted with barley in early summer, and as we passed up the second of the fields, we were literally 'dive-bombed' by a pair of lapwings, who must have been nesting at the edge of the field. At the end of these fields, take a sharp right to pass in front of the stables, and then turn left down the tarmac road. Shortly, you will see a footpath sign on your right, where you pass through a kissing gate, and cross the field ahead, passing a couple of fishing ponds (there are usually two or three donkeys in the field, but they totally ignore you). Climb over a very wobbly stile and then, shortly after, an even ricketier one. You emerge on a country road and turn right past some very large new houses. In the left-hand corner look for a footpath sign, follow down the alley, then take the right of two stiles, to pass through a field of sheep. Pass over another two stiles and on the farm road after the second turn left. Shortly, you will go right along another track. After only thirty yards, pass to the side of a gate, and turn right again, to follow a well-defined path, with pastureland opening out before you: barley to the left and wheat to the right on our walk. (You have briefly left Wigan Borough to take a short passage through an area of Bolton... not all walks can be perfect.)

At the end of the crop fields you cross a bridge, and carry on along the side of fencing, until you reach a wooden kissing gate, which comes out onto Wigan Road. Cross the busy road and follow the footpath sign just to your left, where you again pass a field of donkeys. Descend to a bridge over an 'Ockery brook'... You may have to walk the plank if it has rained (you'll know what I mean when you get there). Turn right along a wooded trail, that seems to form a tunnel, and is almost deafening with birdsong. When you reach a metal gate, you are faced with three paths, and you will take the middle one. (The one to the left proceeds to Howe Bridge Crematorium and can add a very enjoyable and picturesque two-mile return trek, if you so wished.) Along that middle path you continue as it rises and falls through pretty woodlands, and eventually emerges opposite Westleigh High School.

Turn right along Westleigh Lane, and after six hundred yards, locate a footpath sign on the left-hand side of the road, where you pass through a metal squeeze stile, and follow the disused railway track. For some reason, there is an abundance of wild roses along the sides of the track. You pass a large flash on your left, popular with local anglers, and the track tends to get rather muddy and wet from here.

It comes out onto Leigh Road, which you cross and then you follow another footpath directly opposite. This is the site of the former Hindley Green Railway Station, now a block of flats. Go down the tricky downhill slope (the track at the bottom is again often quite muddy... dirt bikers?). Follow this track for maybe two hundred yards, then take an uphill track on your right, which emerges onto grassy fields. Follow the grassy trail diagonally right, looking for a modern white building on your right (Thomas St. School). Veer to your right and pass to the left of the school, through a stile, and cross the back of a football pitch, known locally as Hindley Green Rec. Continue up the path, then the joining road, to reach Atherton Road again. The Swan Hotel is just on your right. Your journey's end drink awaits you.

Walk 3

Abram, Bickershaw and Hindley Green

Distance: 7 miles
Time: 3.5 hours

Terrain: Pretty good throughout. A mixture of stony and grassy paths.

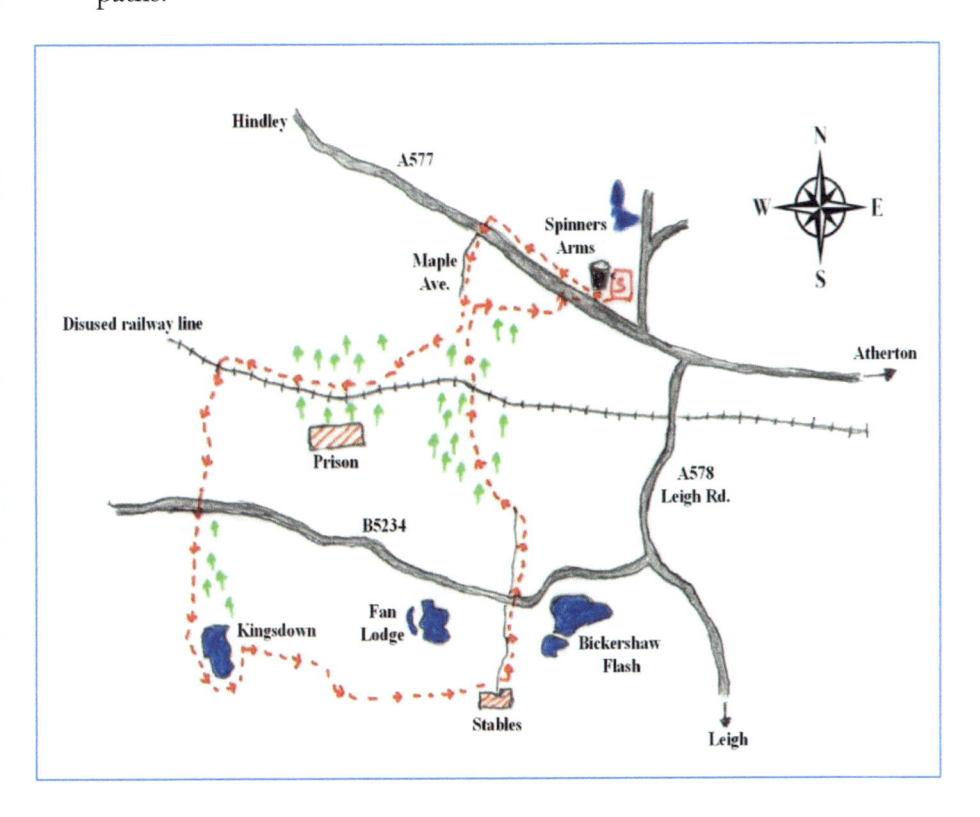

Our starting (and finishing) point is the Spinners Arms on Atherton Road (A577), Hindley Green. With the pub to your back, head right up Atherton Road, passing a row of shops on your left. One hundred yards on, turn left up Maple Ave (formerly Scowcroft Street, named after the pit that was situated at the end of the street). At the end, the road continues onto a dirt track. The field on the right was once the equivalent of Old Trafford and Central Park in my youth, and many a cup final was played there (probably too much competition from Xboxes today). The track bends right past Close Lane Farm, and then left. Shortly you take a path on your right, past a couple of houses and a stables. At the end of this track, go left and immediately right through a metal gate, to follow a shaded woodland path that follows the disused railway line. Through the trees on your left you can see HM Borstal, Hindley.

Stay on this path, ignoring the various offshoots, for around a mile. It's a very pleasant path; another example of nature reclaimed from the mining industry. When last walked, we almost stood on a weasel as it shot out of the undergrowth and scurried across our path. As the path opens up to grassed land, the field on the left contained several shire horses, and further on, a number of rusty trailers and machinery. You reach a tarmac road at the end and turn left up to Bickershaw Lane. Cross the road and turn right then left up a bridle path. This is another lovely path that climbs gently to the rear of Abram. You cross a shale track and continue to Kingsdown Flash (known locally as 'Polly's'). Go through the gate on your right to circumnavigate the flash. It's worth taking some time to fully appreciate these waters: home to anglers, bird watchers and nature lovers. As you reach the end of the flash, look for footpath signs on the left of the road, and take the middle one of three paths, with the lake and a wooden fence on your left. You soon arrive at a small bridge and turn right onto the shale track you crossed earlier. Follow this track to a metal gate, and go past the post stile, continuing up the field ahead.

Waymarker signs guide you up the side of another two fields, before the yellow arrows take you on a little detour through a small wooded copse (and some very sharp brambles), over a 'hardly there' stile, and then left along the edge of another pasture. As you look to your left, you see the fields of Bickershaw spread out before you. This was the site of the 'famous' Bickershaw Pop Festival of 1972, which featured The Kinks, Donovan and American rock legends The Grateful Dead. Continue along this line, eventually descending to a large new house and extensive stabling. Pass through the stable yard and turn left along the road past the eyesore that was once a *small* scrap metal yard. This lane merges onto Bolton House Road, with the former miners' terraced houses on your right, and the long gone Bickershaw Cricket Club on your left. At the top, cross the main road, and follow straight ahead up Rivington Drive, to locate a metal gate in the top left-hand corner.

Follow this track until you reach a crossroad of tracks, where you turn right onto a track that eventually merges onto Close Lane, where we began the walk. (This is an area where deer are regularly sighted amidst the long grasses and light forest along the edge of the track.) As you begin to reach the end of Close Lane, look for a small opening through the trees on your right, and follow the path to emerge at the top of Oak Avenue. Turn right, then follow the road diagonally left, through the bungalows to come back to Atherton Road. Aldi faces you, as you turn right, and return to the Spinners Arms.

Cliff Peters

Walk 4

Flashes, Locks and Rugby Clubs

Distance: 5.5 miles
Time: 2.5 hours

Terrain: Good footpaths and paved canal sides

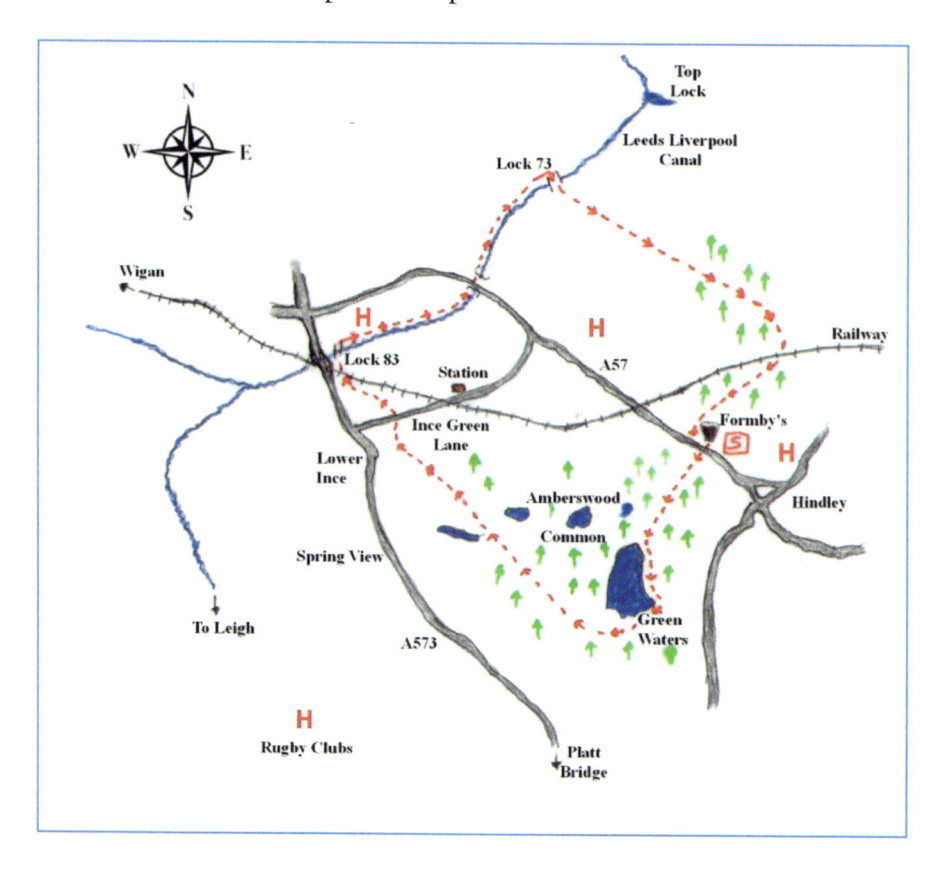

Thiswalk begins at Formby's pub (formerly Hockery Brook, and Amberswood Inn) on the A577, heading out of Hindley towards Wigan. From Hindley, it crosses Amberswood Common, through Lower Ince, Rose Bridge and Higher Ince. The area is a mixture of canalside and nature reserve.

Park opposite Formby's on the small car park and walk through the gate behind you heading towards Amberswood Nature Reserve. After about a mile of pleasant walking, you reach the first of several waters in the area. This is known as 'The Greenwaters' and was an exceptional angling water in my youth (many large pike in particular being netted on the water). Continue along the left of the lake, observing the abundance of waterfowl, including heron, grebe, coot and swan. Around the top edge of the lake follow the footpath sign marked 'Ince'. You will notice the totem pole at the pathside (obviously belonging to the Platt Bridge Arapaho tribe), and other carvings. Continue along the main pathway, passing other small man-made lakes. Ignore the paths leading off to left and right (though they are well worth exploring on future visits, which I have no doubt you will make). You will shortly reach a green metal bridge across a stream, after which the track swings right and emerges at a gate in front of a grassed area.

Passing a row of terraced houses, you come to Ince Green Lane, which you cross and pick up the footpath directly opposite. The former Manley pub is on your right, and you continue, under the railway bridge, to reach the Leeds/Liverpool canal at lock 83. Cross the canal bridge, and turn right along the Leeds/Liverpool canal, along a slightly ascending path which culminates at 'Top Lock'. This stretch of canal is home to twenty one locks over a two-mile and 200-foot climb, (more per mile than any other part of its 102 miles). On your left, you shortly pass Wigan St. Patricks R.L. Club (famous for producing countless R.L stars, including Andy Gregory, Joe Lydon and Joe Egan). Half a mile along this well-kept path, you cross Manchester Road at Rose Bridge (the rugby club of the same name, and another R.L. stronghold is a few hundred yards to your right) with Bill Ashurst and Ryan Sutton amongst their former players.

Continue along the canalside, passing yet more locks. A pair of yellow wagtails seemed to follow us along this stretch, as they hunted insects for their young. Upon reaching lock 73, it is unfortunately time to leave the canal, though 'Top Lock' is not much further on and can easily be included if you so desire. Cross the canal bridge here and pass through the metal kissing gate to follow the path on the opposite side. This tree-lined path is another recent addition to the Wigan network, and it soon crosses Belle Green Lane at the former Bush Hotel (once run by the famous Billy Boston). You pass the former Morrison's supermarket on the right and pass under the railway bridge soon after (Hindley R.L. and Cricket Club can now be seen on your left; a more recent addition to the local sporting clubs, but certainly with impressive facilities). Paul Deacon and Paul Johnson were G.B. players from the club.

The end of the walk is now imminent as you descend back to the main road.

Hope you enjoyed it!

Walk 5

Adlington and Worthington Lakes

Distance: 7 miles
Time: 3.00 Hours

Terrain: Good tracks along derelict railway lines (can be muddy at times), excellent canal towpaths, and woodland. Only one steep climb.

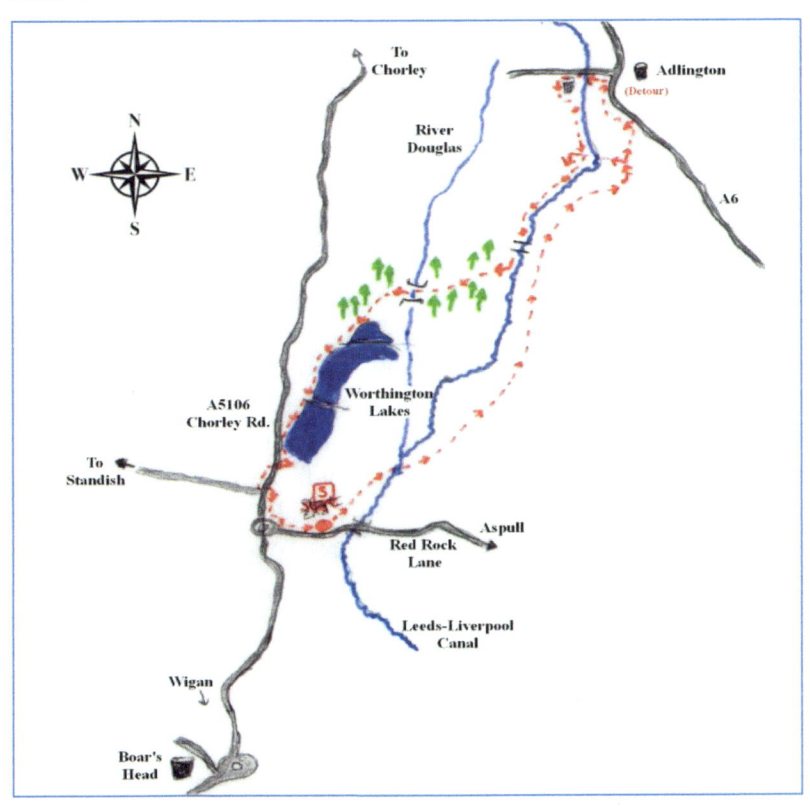

A delightful and unusual walk, passing through varied countryside, which actually meanders out of the borough for a while (though only for a short time).

The starting point is the car park on the right of Red Rock Lane, fifty yards after you go over the canal bridge, and past the former Crawford Arms, heading towards Standish. The footpath is in the right-hand corner of the car park, and it follows the former railway track. You soon pass the 'Old Station House', built on the site of the Standish Union Station, and the track continues under the Leeds Liverpool canal. Whilst this path can be muddy at times, it's a lovely, wooded path, and the sounds of several songbirds accompany you along the whole stretch. The track swings gently to the left, and you soon begin to spy the canal running parallel, some two hundred yards on your left. Along the two miles or so of this path, you pass through three relatively new gates, and at the end of the track, you descend to the River Douglas, where you turn left, and shortly after climb right up some steps to join the canal itself. You now turn right onto the towpath heading back towards Wigan. However, there were major N.W.W.A works here, when we walked the route, and we had to bypass the track to the river and take the farm track to the main road. Turn left along here, left again at the White Bull, and left onto the canal at the Bridge Inn, some six hundred yards further along (hopefully this won't be necessary).

Whichever route you took, you will now be heading along the canal towards Wigan, and you should really enjoy this picturesque length of water and the abundance of wildlife on it. (In May, there was a pair of nesting swans on the opposite bank with six cygnets, as well as several nesting geese.) After passing bridge 63, keep your eyes open for a footpath sign on your right some eight hundred yards ahead. Take this path and follow it as it meanders downhill and slightly left, through some fairly dense woodland. A large fallen tree which blocks the path had been cut back by the foresters, to form an archway, as it was obviously too large to move. You will soon begin to hear the sound of the River Douglas, gushing down the narrow valley below, and spot the green metal bridge crossing the river.

Turn left along the path, and soon you will pass through a gate into Worthington Reservoir Country Park (a magnificent area constructed in the late 19th century and containing a number of lakes that feed the Wigan water systems). Take the path along the right of the first lake and continue along this side of the rest of the lakes. Take some time to enjoy the beauty of the area, and the great variety of birdlife that frequent the waters (grebe, cormorant, heron, and several species of geese and duck are common sights). As you pass the last of the lakes, the Kilhey Court Hotel, and the Lakeside Care Home, appear on the right. Soon after, take the track to your left, to emerge at a car park on Chorley Road. Turn left onto the A5106, and alas, begin a mile or so of road walking, which culminates in the only real climb of the walk.

You pass the old 'Bleachworks' on your left, and its remaining frontal facade (heritage or eyesore?), past the new housing estate on the left, and soon after, you come to a mini roundabout. Turn left here, up Red Rock Lane, which climbs steeply back to the car park. Unusually, this walk doesn't end at a public house, but you are (I assure you), less than a mile from the Boar's Head, at the top of Wigan Lane, or several other options in nearby Standish.

Walk 6

Fairies, Pheasants and Football

Distance: 8 miles
Time: 3.5 hours

Terrain: Mostly good paths, and tracks, but can be muddy in places.

Starting Point: Near to Appley Bridge Station or the Waterside pub, both close to Appley Lane North.

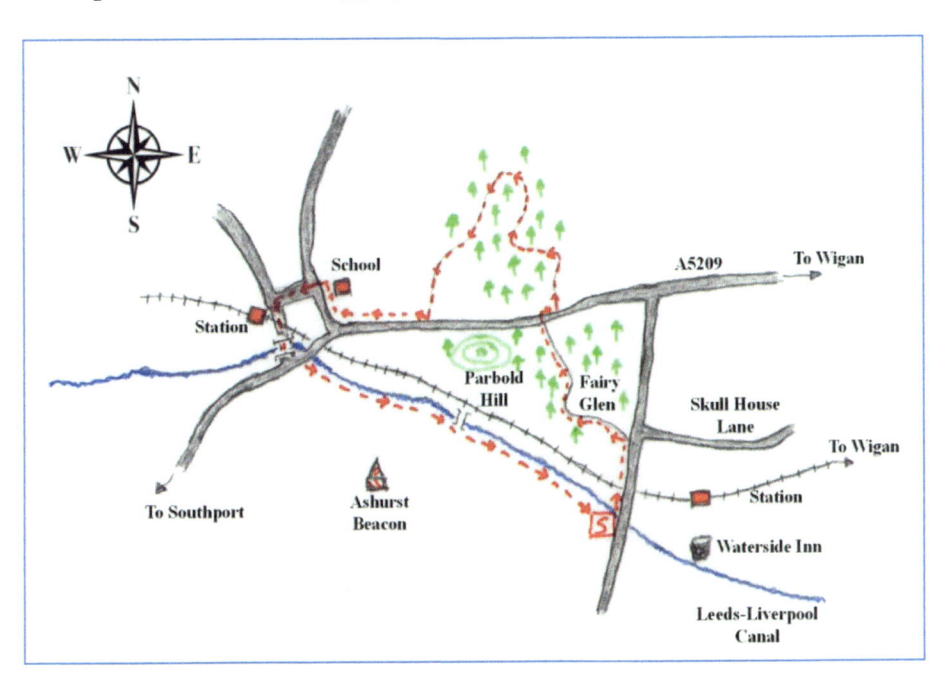

Whilst the walk does pass through areas outside the borough, I feel it is worth doing so to fully explore an outstanding area of natural beauty. We begin with a gentle ascent of Appley Lane North, until we reach Skull House Lane on the right. A footpath sign on the left leads us up a track past some pleasant cottages. The track passes through fields and provides a stunning view over Douglas Valley to the left. Continue, after leaving this fern-bordered track onto another track, which bears right and then left up a well-trodden dirt path. Go down a few steps and cross a tarmac road onto another grassy path. At the end, near an ongoing barn conversion, go over a stile at the side of a metal gate, turn right, and shortly after, turn left through a squeeze stile into 'Fairy Glen'.

This is a unique little wooded area, where there is indeed much evidence of 'fairy activity', in the form of tree doorways, coin logs and glitter trails (my two youngest granddaughters love these woods). As I entered the Glen, I was immediately struck by the smell of wild garlic, and in a murky little pond on the right, I was surprised to see a yellow wagtail skittering across the water. There is no right or wrong way to pass through the Glen, but if you continue in roughly the same direction along the main track (over bridges and rivulets), you will arrive at the exit up an incline in the north corner. The main objective is to enjoy it.

Cross the busy A5209, head right to the car park on the right, and locate a stile at the side of a gate in the corner. Follow the path up the field, and upon reaching another gate, turn left following a wall on your right. At the end of the wall, cross a stile and a rickety bridge, to begin a pleasant though often muddy trek between a fenced area and a stream (the area to the left was full of dozens of young pheasant scrambling around on the other side of the fence). Cross a couple more stiles and 'bridges', until reaching the end of this woodland area at some fields. Continue in the same direction up a grassy track, heading for a white house in the distance. Go round the right side of the house to emerge onto a metalled road (an impressive looking house titled Long Mead will be facing you).

Turn left up this road, and keep to the left, as it turns into a grassy lane descending towards Parbold Hill (you should be able to spot Ashurst Beacon in the far distance). Over a stile by a metal gate, and another by a wooden gate, you then bear right towards a wooded area ahead. Up on reaching this, turn left alongside of the wood and continue downhill to a stile in the corner of the field. Follow the path over a stream via a broken wooden bridge, and up the path to reach the A5209 again. You barely touch the road, however, as you immediately take the tarmac path on your right to descend past some rather expensive looking houses (one with a very impressive man-made waterfall). You reach Lancaster Lane, turn right past a school and a convent, where you take the road on the left: Tan House Lane. Continue along here, until reaching the village centre of Parbold. Go on past the shops, and then the railway station until you come to the canal bridge which is crossed on the left-hand side of the road. You then follow the facing canal to your right, heading back towards Wigan.

You now commence a 2.5 mile walk along one of the most delightful stretches of the Leeds/Liverpool canal. At the beginning of this stretch, you will see that several of the canalside properties have taken advantage of the outstanding views and landscaped their gardens right down to the water's edge. Enjoy this leisurely walk along the wide, wooded and reeded stretch of the canal to pass the 99-mile marker for Leeds. There are normally several narrowboats and barges enjoying this very wide stretch of canal, and several species of waterfowl also. At Gillibrand bridge, you will observe the River Douglas running alongside very close on your right. As you approach a row of cottages near a lock, you are ready to leave the canal by the bridge and return to Appley Lane North and your car. I'm sure that drink at the Waterside (a lovely canalside inn), will be more than welcome.

You may be wondering about the relevance of the football part of the walk title. Well, shortly after completing the walk and listening to the radio, I heard the terrible news that our Wigan Athletic Club had gone into administration (almost spoiled the walk).

Walk 7

Bridgewater Canal and Pennington Flash

Distance: 7 miles
Time: 3.5 hours

Terrain: Excellent paths throughout the walk. Can be muddy around Appletree Stables.

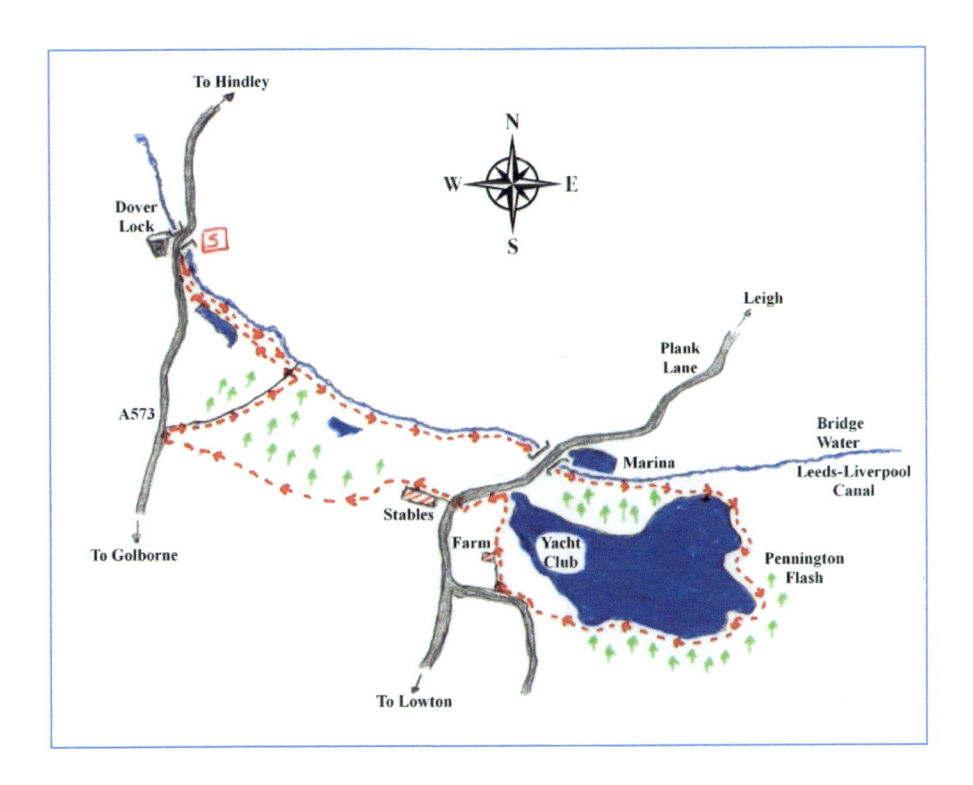

Cliff Peters

A very pleasant and flat walk, taking in the Leigh side of the borough.
You begin at the Dover Lock Inn on the canal bridge where the A573 crosses the canal. Park just over the canal bridge on the left, and, facing the canal, head off to your right, with the canal on your left. The canal is an offshoot of the Leeds/Liverpool, and eventually meets up with the Manchester Ship Canal past Worsley (the stretch between Pennington and Worsley is actually well worth walking). You soon pass Lightshaw Flash on your right-hand side; a picturesque stretch of water, which, when we passed in mid-June, was alive with dozens of swallows, swooping to catch insects off the surface. Shortly you pass three information boards, depicting the industrial heritage of the region and soon after bridges five and six.

After 1.5 miles, you reach Plank Lane Marina and lift bridge. This is built near the site of the former Plank Lane Colliery, dating back to 1872. Cross Plank Lane and continue along the canal past the new canal side housing that has been developed since the construction of the marina in 2012. The growth of housing around the area has been massive, though to be fair, tasteful. Shortly you will pass two man-made memorials to the area's coal mining heritage (one of which is the remains of an old pit shaft). At the metal bridge No. 9, leave the canal and take the stony path into Pennington Flash Country Park. You stay on this path, following the circumference of the lake; passing bird hides (well worth

visiting if you are something of a twitcher), past the children's playground, and then the car park, with the lake always on your right. This path continues around the lake, which is a haven for anglers, sailors and birdwatchers (amongst the small sailing boats, there were several paddle boarders when we passed). Eventually, you emerge at a metal gate and onto a tarmac road, which passes the Leigh and Lowton Yacht Club, reaching a main road at Lowton Common.

Turn right onto this road, and after a bend, you will see a footpath sign after about five hundred yards on your right. Follow this down a farm track, past the farm itself, and along the north edge of the flash. The path ends at Plank Lane, where you turn left along the lane for about six hundred yards. Look for a footpath sign on the right for Appletree Stables, then cross the road and continue along the track. As you approach the stables, follow the arrow markers which divert you around the stables to your right. There were certainly some good-looking horses in the fields (some of which would probably have left my £5 bets at Haydock Park in their wake). These markers will eventually bring you onto a country lane, where you turn right. Just after a gate stile, there is a sign guiding you round a horseshoe-shaped path skirting Lightshaw Meadow. This is a relatively new plantation of lesser-known trees and wild grasses, that abound with butterflies and birds: a worthwhile ten-minute diversion, with some benches available, if you fancy a coffee.

Back on the original track again, pass through a kissing gate, and then past some very nice barn conversions, soon reaching the main A573 road. You aren't on it very long, as almost immediately, there is another footpath sign on your right. Through the kissing gate, follow this grit track that is bordered with wild daisies along its entire length (if you are startled by the sound of shotgun along here, it will be from the shooting estate on the left). This path is the remains of another disused mining railway line and ends as it began, at a kissing gate. Rise up the slope on the left and rejoin the canal, turning left to complete the last half-mile stretch back to the starting point.

If the Dover Lock is closed (as it was after our walk), head back towards Abram and the Buck's Head.

Walk 8

Water, water everywhere (Viridor Woods and the Canal)

Distance: 6 miles
Time: 2.5 hours

Terrain: Generally good, though some stretches can be awkward in bad weather.

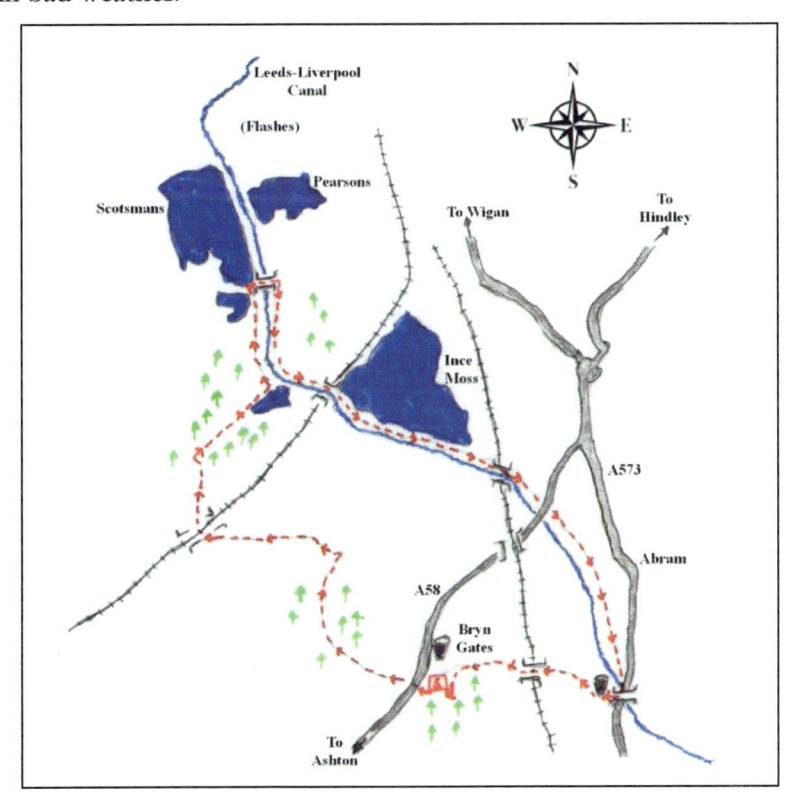

Start the walk from the car park on the left of the A58 heading towards Ashton, just after the Bryn Gates Hotel (the second of two areas). Leave the car park and cross over the A58 (Lily Lane), following a footpath sign immediately opposite. You soon pass through a pretty wooded area, which leads to a sign for Viridor Woods. Here you bear left and then right along a track through more recently planted trees (The Three Sisters area is straight ahead). You will shortly approach some large green compost recycling sheds (You'll probably smell them before you see them!), and to the right of those look for a row of quaint, white, terraced houses. Turn left as you reach these houses along a wide stony track and continue past some much larger houses. The track widens out as it passes through agricultural fields, planted with barley when we walked it last.

After passing over a large metal railway bridge, keep your eyes open for a track on your right-hand side which is accessed through a metal gate at the side of a massive concrete 'polo mint'. You follow this trail for about 1.5 miles, as it continues on a slightly downhill course. On the day we walked it, we got caught in a mid-June downpour, and the track resembled a small river (we two were the 'drowned rats'). Keep to this path, passing a heavily fenced storage area; ignoring various cycle paths to both left and right. Soon you pass a large flash on your right, the first of many over the next few miles. You reach the Leeds/Liverpool canal shortly after, and though you need to head right towards Leigh, we must first go left as there is no access along this bank.

Follow this path to Bridge No. 2, and

cross to the opposite side. As you cross this bridge, the impressive Scotsman's Flash is on your left; a hub of sailing activity throughout the year. On the other side, turn right and follow this wonderful stretch of canal for almost two miles, as it passes through Spring View, Ince, Bamfurlong and Abram. The area is also a mass of flashes, yet another result of our coal-mining heritage, caused by subsidence, and resultant flooding from the mines (there are eight main flashes in the Wigan area, though several more smaller ones). As we approached Ince Moss Flash on your left, we were greeted by a cacophony of noise, from the various waterfowl nesting on the mud islands in the flash, and on its edges. Pass under Bamfurlong Bridge on Lily Lane and continue along the canal towpath until you reach the Dover Lock pub on your right.

Leave the canal and locate the footpath sign at the side of the pub. It crosses a bridge over a small stream, then crosses the fields ahead, diagonally right. Pass a few more, smaller waterways, and head for the railway bridge in front of you. Pass under the bridge, to face distinct footpaths to the right and left (if you want to extend this walk by a mile or so, take the left path, and follow this along a pretty wooded path, which eventually swings right and ends up back at our starting point). For this walk, you go right, and continue along the path as it zigzags through freshly planted woodland along Ashton Moss. You soon reach a memorial plaque, set into a large stone, on your left. This was erected in memory of a local miner named Bill Jones. Take the right fork here, and after a further two hundred yards, proceed left along a grassy path to soon reach the car park and the end of the walk.

The Bryn Gates is the obvious choice of watering hole, though Ashton town centre is only a couple of miles along the A58, if the first place is not open.

Walk 9

Wigan's Royalty Walk

Distance: 6 miles
Time: 2.5 hours

Terrain: Generally good, though the tracks around Lady Mabel's Wood can get quite muddy.

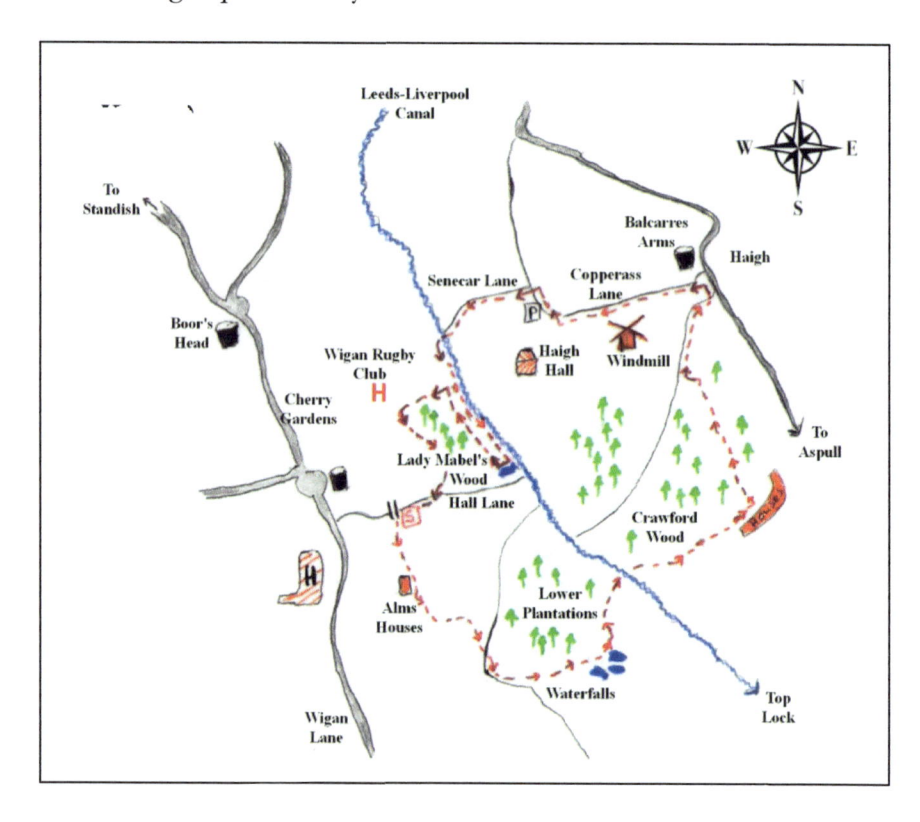

A lovely walk through woodland, Haigh Hall Plantations and a stretch of canal. You come across plenty of royalty in the guise of Lady Mabel, Lord Crawford, Lord Haigh and the Earl of Balcarres.

Begin the walk on Hall Lane; reached via Leyland Mill Lane off Wigan Lane between the hospital and the Cherry Gardens pub (your closest watering hole). Park in the lay-by on your right, just before an old former railway bridge, and take the lane on the left just back from the lay-by. The unmade road passes through fields on either side, to reach converted Alms Houses (these were built in 1772 to house 'respected' employees of the Haigh Estate and are grade 2 listed). Follow the steps in the corner, turning left at the bottom into the Lower Plantations. Follow this path, crossing a bridge, and then turn right where it joins the main track. This continues downhill, and veers left at a bench on your left-hand side.

Upon reaching a man-made waterfall, follow the steep steps up the side of the falls. The path climbs steadily up to the Aspull Sough water treatment ponds; make sure to ignore any track to the left or right (these ponds filter and clean water contaminated by iron pyrite, from former mining works, before it flows down to the River Douglas). After the last of these three ponds, turn left and follow the path over the canal, which then veers slightly to the right and then straight ahead into Crawford Woods.

At an intersection of paths, keep to the right towards a gate with houses beyond. Don't leave the wood but take the grassy path on your right following the line of houses on your right. This path passes through woodland until it reaches another track, where you turn right. You pass the cemetery and the church of St. David (built in 1830); turn left onto the main road, and then left at the Balcarres Arms pub down Copperas Lane, heading into Haigh Hall. You pass St. David's school (built in 1845), and soon reach Haigh Windmill on your left, which was originally used to pump water to John Summers Brewery, also built in 1845, but long defunct (the windmill was in a poor condition for many years but was restored some years ago by some local businessmen, inc. the late Tom Bibby).

If you have not had the pleasure of seeing the magnificent building and grounds of Haigh Hall, continue straight on through the barrier, and do so at your leisure (the Hall was built in 1830 by James Lindsey, the Earl of Balcarres). The road swings right at the barrier, past the car park and shortly afterwards, you turn left down Sennicar Lane. Descend steeply through the golf course, where you will appreciate great views of the Douglas Valley unfolding before you. On reaching the Leeds/Liverpool canal, cross the bridge, go through the gate on the left, and proceed along this pretty stretch of waterway. This length is one of the best on the canal to spot kingfishers, so keep your eyes on the opposite reedy bank.

The next path is on your right, just before a hump-backed bridge. Go through the kissing gate ahead and follow the path to the right, circling the outside of Lady Mabel's Wood (this area is particularly well known for its Roe Deer population, so keep your eyes open). You will pass a couple of benches, and as you come to an intersection of paths, go straight ahead on the grassy and rather muddy path. At the northern edge of the woods, you reach another bench in a clearing and track left through a wooded area, which opens up to fields on your right (you should also be able to see Wigan R.U. Club on your right). Continue through this attractive forested area, to arrive at a fence. Veer left, and shortly after, turn right at a junction. Follow this track until you reach a wooden gate at the end. Go through this gate, turn right, and you will locate your car further down Hall Lane.

Walk 10

Standish Circular

Distance 6.5 miles
Time: 3 hours

Terrain: Mostly good tracks, even after some heavy rain. Some road walking but a very enjoyable walk around the environs of Standish.

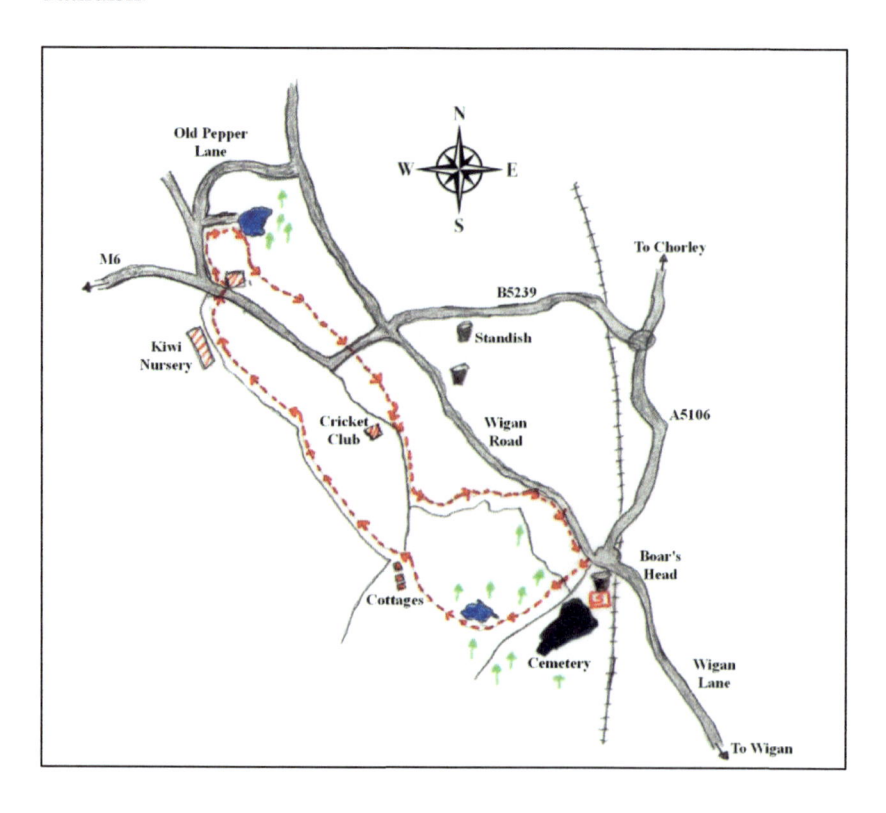

You begin at Gidlow Cemetery on Wigan Road, close to the Boar's Head pub. Park here and then walk back to the cemetery gates, turning immediately left along a country lane. Continue along this hawthorn-edged lane until you reach a gate in front of a large farm, where you climb over the stile on your immediate right and follow this path through fields of barley. This area and beyond was once home to several coal mines, including Gidlow and Giant's Hall pits (there were over twenty mines in this area at the start of the 20th century). Shortly you take another stile on your left and follow this path as it takes you around a large square field. At the far end of this field, a stile on your right guides you along another path, resplendent with bright yellow rape seed flowers on both sides. If you look to your left as you walk, you have an open vista of the Douglas valley, with the enormous Heinz complex clearly visible.

At the next stile, you veer right along a track, passing some very old stone cottages, which were undergoing restoration at the time. Once past these cottages, turn immediately left, and proceed along the track, shortly passing the Windmill Brewery on your left, and the Bowling Green Farm on your right. You emerge onto Arbour Lane and follow the road to the right past the Kiwi Nurseries, and out onto the A5209. Cross the road to the Brittania Hotel (formerly the well-known Cassinelli's), going to your left. Turn right into Old Pepper Lane, and right again shortly after into Brookfield Lane. At the end of this street is a very pretty fishing lake, where we had a coffee on one of the picnic benches. However, the path we are taking is on the right just before the lake. This joins a red shale path known as 'The Line', which passes behind Wigan Road. and follows the course of an old railway line. After about a mile, with the busy Standish centre approaching, take the road on the right through some houses, and then left along Witham Close. You emerge on School Lane, just at the side of the recently established Albert's restaurant.

Cross School Lane at the crossing and continue straight across up Green Lane. After passing a school and an old folks' home, you reach the end of the lane. Bear right past some ancient water towers, and upon reaching Standish Cricket Club, go left up Standish Wood Lane. Pass Strickland House on your left, and shortly after, take the footpath sign on your left. There is a farm on your right as you continue along the path behind housing, which culminates at Hartington Drive. You will hear and see the busy Wigan Road ahead, and you turn right onto it, and proceed the last half mile to your starting point. The excellent Boars Head awaits.

The actual walk is over upon reaching the cemetery, but as the pubs had still not reopened following lockdown, we decided to visit an old friend, lost to us almost exactly ten years ago. A great mate, and a proper Wiganer: R.I.P. Kevin Ashton.

THE AUTHOR

Cliff would describe himself as a 'born and bred' Wiganer, having lived in the town all his life (apart from a short spell as a baby), and NEVER wished to live anywhere else. Born in 1954, he was educated at Sacred Heart R.C Primary School in Hindley Green, Thornleigh College in Bolton (not the best years of his life .... they didn't even play rugby!) and Wigan Technical College.

His first job was at Hindley U.D.C as a rates clerk then, following local government re-organisation, progressed to Wigan M.B.C as an auditor. From that point he became a Licensed Trade Stocktaker, initially with Greenall Whitleys, and for the last 30 years was self-employed. This has involved spending a great deal of his working life (and quite a bit of personal life too) in pubs, clubs and restaurants ... not a bad working life.

An ardent rugby fan, Cliff was an enthusiastic (if average) playing member of Wigan R.U.F.C for almost 25 years and loved every minute of it. He was also a pretty successful junior Rugby League coach for over 15 years with both the Wigan Schools and Hindley A.R.L.F.C; and several future stars of the game benefited from his coaching; including recently retired Wigan R. L captain, Sean O'Loughlin, and former International players, Paul Deacon and Paul Johnson. He has always been a big fan of Wigan Rugby League Club and rugby league in general. Unlike many rugby fans in the town, he also follows the football team and was at Wembley to see them win the F.A Cup in that unbelievable 2013 final.

Married to Lynn for 47 years he has 2 children; Michael and Kerry, and 4 grandchildren; Will, Jessica, Layla and Hallie, all of whom have experienced, though not always enjoyed, at least one of Grandad's walks.

Unfortunately, shortly after completing this book, Cliff suffered significant sight loss due to a long standing health condition. He is now classed as partially sighted so the emphasis on personal safety has diminished his appreciation of the countryside a little, although he still manages to get out for walks on a regular basis. He is passionate about his town and hopes that this book will encourage people to explore it fully. Not just the walks illustrated in the book but other surrounding areas not covered. There is so much more about the Wigan area than is initially apparent and the benefits to be gained from discovering them are immense. 'Wigan really is Wonderful'.

BV - #0002 - 240221 - C27 - 210/148/2 - PB - 9781913839086